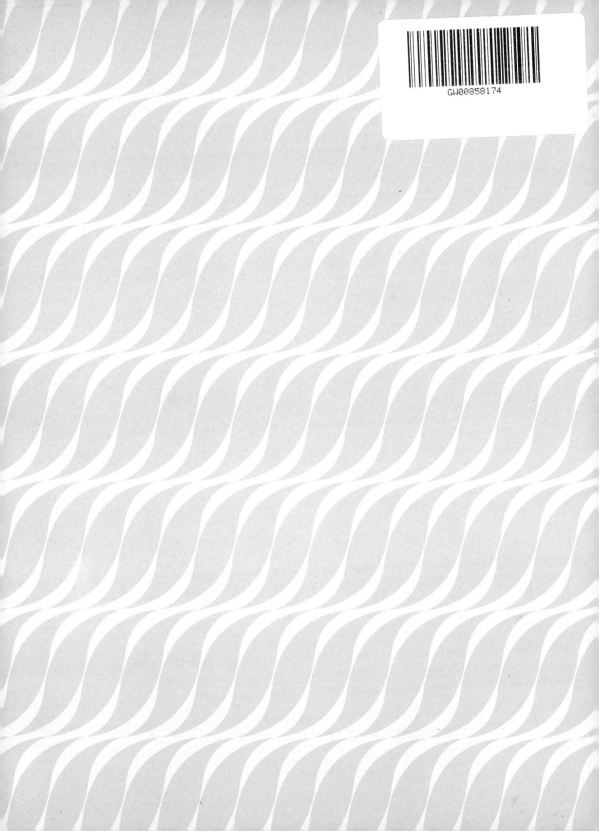

All About
MACHINES

Chris Oxlade
CONSULTANT Graham Peacock

southwater

This edition is published by Southwater

Southwater is an imprint of Anness Publishing Ltd

Hermes House, 88–89 Blackfriars Road, London SE1 8HA

tel. 020 7401 2077; fax 020 7633 9499

info@anness.com

© Anness Publishing Limited 2001, 2002

Published in the USA by Southwater, Anness Publishing Inc.

27 West 20th Street, New York, NY 10011; fax 212 807 6813

This edition distributed in the UK by The Manning Partnership

tel. 01225 852 727; fax 01225 852 852; sales@manning-partnership.co.uk

This edition distributed in the USA by National Book Network

tel. 301 459 3366; fax 301 459 1705; www.nbnbooks.com

This edition distributed in Canada by General Publishing

tel. 416 445 3333; fax 416 445 5991; www.genpub.com

This edition distributed in Australia by Pan Macmillan Australia

tel. 1300 135 113; fax 1300 135 103; email customer.service@macmillan.com.au

This edition distributed in New Zealand by The Five Mile Press (NZ) Ltd

tel. (09) 444 4144; fax (09) 444 4518; fivemilenz@clear.net.nz

A CIP catalogue record for this book is available from the British Library.

Publisher: Joanna Lorenz

Managing Editor, Children's Books: Linda Fraser

Editors: Charlotte Evans, Louisa Somerville

Photographer: John Freeman

Designers and Illustrator: Caroline Grimshaw, Joyce Mason, Nick Hawken

The Publishers would like to thank the following children, and their parents, for appearing
in this book – Nana Addae, Maria Bloodworth, Ricky Edward Garrett, Sasha Haworth,
Alex Lindblom-Smith, Sophie Lindblom-Smith, Laura Masters, Jessica Moxley,
Aidan Mulcahy, Fiona Mulcahy, Seán Mulcahy, Jamie Rosso and Joe Westbrook.

Picture credits: Ancient Egypt Picture Library:18tr, 18b. Bruce Coleman Ltd: 32bl, 32br, 33tl;
/M Borchi 15tr; /G Clyde 25c; /Gryniewicz 56bl; /J Jurka 11c; /H Lange 5tr; /N McAllister 15cl;
/HP Merton 57bl. Ecoscene: 32c, 49bl; /N Hawkes 19bl, 48bl; /W Lawler 20cl; /M Maidment 51tl;
/Towse 52tr. E.T. Archive 15tl, 24b, 46tr, 48tr, 53bl, 55t. Mary Evans Picture Library: 29br, 32tr.
Hold Studios: /I Belcher 50bl; /A Burridge 22c, 53br; /N Cattlin 48br, 50br, 50tr, 51tr; /J Hall
20c; /W Harinck 49tr; /P McCullagh 7bl; /P Peacock 56tl; /I Spence 25bl, 51c. ICCE: /M Boulton
5bl. Image Bank:19tr. Powerstock: /Alex Bartel 33bl. Quadrant: 8br, 15br, 15c, 19tl, 24bl, 25br,
37tr, 39c, 41bl, 47br, 49c. Planet Earth Pictures: 5br, 19br. Science Photo Library: 58cl, 61cl;
/M Bond 28c, 47t; /M Fielding 5t; /V Fleming 29br; /P Fletcher 36tr; /Food & Drug Administration
56b; /A Hart-Davis 25tr; /S Horrel 33br; /M Kage 58bl; /J King-Holmes 38tr; /S Ogden 59bl;
/A Pasieka 30c; /Rosenfield Images Ltd 57br; /V Steger 56c, 58cc, 59cl; /US Department of Energy
60tr. Science Museum/Science & Society Picture Library: 14br, 29bl, 36bl, 37c, 43tr, 47c, 54br,
54bl. Tony Stone Images: 39tl; /Agri Press 12bl; /W Bilenduke 40c; /S Egan 5c; /B Lewis 51br;
/P McArthur 43bl; /A Meshkinger 43c; /C Thatcher 43tl; /T Vine 26c. Superstock: 4tr, 5tl, 6br,
26tr, 33c, 49br. Zefa 39br.

Previously published as: Investigations Machines

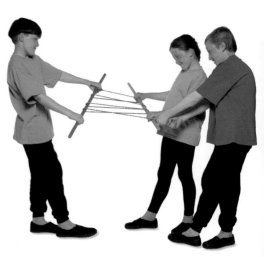

10 9 8 7 6 5 4 3 2 1

MACHINES

CONTENTS

WHAT IS A MACHINE?

Thousands of different devices can be called machines, from calculators and televisions to trucks and aircraft. Scissors and staplers are very simple machines, while computers and cars are complicated. All machines have one thing in common—they help us do jobs and therefore make our lives easier.

Think about what you did yesterday. Make a list of every machine you can remember that you used or saw, from when you woke up to when you went back to bed. Many things that we take for granted, such as opening a can, cutting paper and tightening a screw, can only be done with a machine. Other jobs, such as washing clothes, used to be done by hand but nowadays are usually done by machine. Machines are being improved—and new ones invented—all the time. We may find that tasks that take a long time today become much easier and faster to do in the future.

screwdriver

pliers

scissors

hammer

Allen keys

Simple machines
Tools such as these are simple machines that are useful to have at home. They each do a task that would be much more difficult without them. Can you think of a job for each tool?

Useful screws
The parts of this model helicopter are attached with screws. The screws are machines because they do the job of holding the helicopter parts in place.

Domestic machines
A microwave oven is one of the many machines that people use at home to make preparing and cooking food quicker and simpler. Other domestic machines include vacuum cleaners and washing machines.

Using tools
This girl uses a spanner to tighten the nuts on her model helicopter. A spanner is a simple tool that is used to tighten up, or undo, nuts. Using the spanner is more efficient than if the girl used her fingers alone, because the spanner can make joints much tighter and more secure.

FACT BOX

• Leonardo da Vinci (1452–1519) was an Italian artist and inventor. He drew plans for machines, such as tanks and aircraft, that were hundreds of years ahead of their time.

• Greek scientist Hero of Alexandria lived in the 1st century A.D. He invented a steam engine, a slot machine and a screw press.

Old farm machines

People use many different machines to help them farm the land in this picture, which was painted in about 1400. Some of the first machines ever invented were used by farmers. At the bottom of the picture is a plow, and halfway up on the right-hand side is a water-wheel. At the top, by a church, is a machine called a shaduf, which was used to raise water from a deep well. Next to the shaduf is a machine that was used for sowing seeds.

Calculating machine

Unlike most of the other machines shown here, a computer does not help lift, move or cut things. Instead it makes life easier by remembering information and doing calculations. Computers help us to work faster and more accurately. They can do amazing work—such as controlling the flight path of a spacecraft.

Construction machines

Diggers and cranes are used on a construction (building) site. These huge machines are clearing the site of rubble before the buildings are restored. Construction machines have powerful engines for moving and lifting heavy loads, such as soil, rocks, steel and concrete.

Travel by machine

To travel from place to place you need a machine to get you there. The space shuttle is a machine that transports people into space. Its powerful rocket engines launch it through Earth's atmosphere. Other transport machines, such as cars and trains, also have engines. Their engines are much less powerful than those on a spacecraft.

Chopping machine

A hand ax is used to chop large logs into smaller pieces. When the woman brings the ax down, the sharp blade slices into the wood, forcing it to split apart. The ax is a simple machine, but it is very effective. It does a job that is impossible to do by hand.

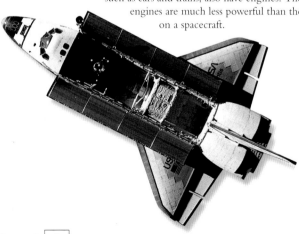

POWERFUL LEVERS

Six simple machines that were invented thousands of years ago are still the basic elements of all machinery. These machines are the lever, the wheel and axle, the inclined plane or ramp, the wedge, the screw and the pulley. The simplest, and probably the oldest, is the lever. A lever is a bar or rod that tilts on an object called a pivot. You only need a small push down on one end to raise a large weight on the end nearer to the pivot. Any rod or stick can act as a lever, helping to move heavy objects or prise things apart. The lever makes the power of the push into a much larger push. This is known as mechanical advantage.

Did you know that some parts of your body are levers? Every time you brush your hair or get up from a chair, the bones in your arms and legs act as levers, helping you to lift your limbs.

Shut the door
Closing a door near the hinge is hard work. It is easier to press on the handle because the door is a lever. Its pivot is made by the hinges. The door turns your small push on the handle into a bigger push.

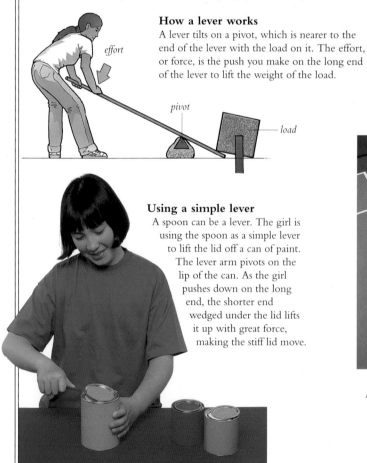

How a lever works
A lever tilts on a pivot, which is nearer to the end of the lever with the load on it. The effort, or force, is the push you make on the long end of the lever to lift the weight of the load.

effort

pivot

— *load*

Using a simple lever
A spoon can be a lever. The girl is using the spoon as a simple lever to lift the lid off a can of paint. The lever arm pivots on the lip of the can. As the girl pushes down on the long end, the shorter end wedged under the lid lifts it up with great force, making the stiff lid move.

Levers in the body
A tennis player uses muscle-powered levers in her shoulders and elbows to serve the ball at high speed. Small movements of the muscles cause large movements of the racket, which gives the racket the speed for a fast serve.

LEVERS AND LIFTING

1 A ruler can be used as a lever to lift a book. With the pivot (the box) near the book, only a small effort is needed to lift the book up. The lever makes the push larger.

2 When the pivot is moved to the middle of the lever, the effort needed to lift the book up is equal to the book's weight. The effort and the load are the same.

3 When the pivot is near where the boy is pressing, more effort is needed to lift the book. The force of the push needed to lift the book is now larger than the book's weight.

Raising water

In Middle Eastern countries, farmers use a machine called a shaduf to lift water to irrigate their crops. The arm of a shaduf is a lever with a bucket on one end and a weight on the other, pivoted on the top of a wooden frame. The shaduf operator pulls the empty bucket down into the water using a rope. The weight at the other end acts as the effort, lifting the bucket of water (the load). The shaduf is an ancient machine, used by farmers for thousands of years.

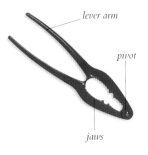

lever arm

pivot

jaws

The strong crushing action of the nutcracker's jaws is produced by pressing the two lever arms together.

Cracking a nut

A pair of nutcrackers, like a pair of scissors or a pair of pliers, has two lever arms joined at a pivot. Pressing the ends of the nutcracker arms together crushes the nut in its jaws. The levers make the effort you use about four times greater, allowing you to break the nut quite easily. Putting the pivot at the end of the levers rather than toward the center (as in a pair of scissors) means that the arms of the cracker can be shorter but still create a force just as great.

BALANCING LEVERS

Levers are used for lifting, cutting and crushing. A lever on a central pivot can also be used as a balance. The lever balances if the effect of the force (push) on one side of the pivot is the same as the effect of the force on the other. A see-saw is one kind of balancing lever. It is a plank balanced on a center post or pivot. Someone small and light can balance a much bigger person if they sit in the right position on a see-saw.

Outside the playground, balancing levers have other important uses. By using a lever to balance one force with another, the size of one force can be compared to the size of another. This is how a weighing machine called a balance scale works. It measures the mass (weight) of an object by comparing it with standard weights such as ounces and pounds.

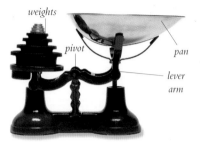

Weighing up
Balance scales like this one were once used for weighing things at stores and in the kitchen. To make the lever arm balance, the weights on the left must equal the weight in the pan.

Using a balance scale
An object, such as a pile of strawberries, is put in a pan resting on one end of the lever arm. Weights are added to the other end of the arm until the arm balances. Then the individual weights are added up to find the weight of the object. We call the result "weight" because we measure the force needed to balance the weight of the object. In fact, a balance scale measures pounds.

Balanced crossing gates
A level-crossing gate is actually a balanced lever. The pivot is at the side of the road, with the gate to one side and a heavy counterweight on the other side to balance it. This means that only a small effort is needed from electric motors to move the lever up or down. The gates are operated automatically by electronics linked to the railway's signalling system.

Two children of equal weight, the same distance from the pivot, make the see-saw balance.

lever arm   pivot

Balancing a see-saw

A see-saw shows the effect of moving a weight nearer or farther from the pivot of a lever arm. Two children of equal weight, the same distance from the pivot, make a see-saw balance. If another child is added to one end, the arm overbalances to that side. By moving the single child farther from the pivot, or the pair closer to it, the arm balances again.

By adding another child to one side, that side overbalances. The pair's greater weight easily lifts the lighter boy.

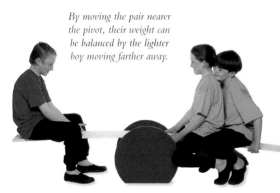

By moving the pair nearer the pivot, their weight can be balanced by the lighter boy moving farther away.

Investigating balance

Make a ruler balance on a tube. Now put different-sized piles of coins at different positions on each end so that they balance. For example, you can make one coin balance two coins if the single coin is twice as far from the pivot as the other coins.

ALL KINDS OF LEVERS

Levers are very common machines. Look around you and see how many levers you can find—don't forget the levers in your own body! Each of the machines shown here has a diagram to show you where the pivot, effort and load are, to help you to see how the lever is working.

Levers are divided into three different basic kinds, or classes. The most common type is a first-class lever, where the pivot is always between the load and the effort, as with a see-saw, a pair of pliers or a spade. In second-class levers, the load is between the pivot and the effort. Nutcrackers and wheelbarrows are examples of these. In a third-class lever, the effort is between the pivot and the load, as with hammers, tweezers and fishing rods.

Spade work
A spade is a first-class lever for lifting and turning soil. A sharp blade makes it easy to push the spade into the soil. Pressing down on the handle is the effort, the pivot is your foot on the blade and the load is the soil. Pushing the handle down levers the soil up.

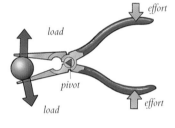

In a pair of pliers, the effort is pressing down on handles. The load is the resistance that an object has to being crushed in the jaws of the pliers.

Lifting the handles of a wheelbarrow lifts a heavy load nearer the pivot, or wheel.

First-class levers
A pair of pliers has two lever arms linked at the pivot by a hinge. They are first-class levers because the pivot is between the load and the effort. The handles are on one side of the pivot and the jaws are on the other.

Second-class levers
A wheelbarrow does not look like a lever, but it is one. The lever arm goes from the end of the handle to the center of the wheel, which is the pivot. A small effort pulling up on the handles lifts the load in the barrow.

A hammer acts as a lever when you use your wrist as a pivot. Your fingers make the effort to lift the hammer's head.

pivot · effort · load

Third-class levers

A hammer may not look like a lever, but it is. The handle joins with your hand to make the lever arm, with your wrist as the pivot. Your fingers supply the effort to make the hammer head move down. The load is the weight of the hammer head. The small movement of your arm makes a large movement in the hammer head to drive the nail into the wood.

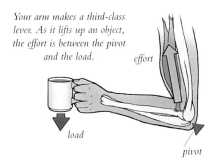

Gone fishing

A fishing rod is a third-class lever, similar to the hammer above. The pivot is at the fisherman's wrist. The effort is made by his hand, and the load is the weight of the rod and the fish on the line. An effort much greater than the load is needed to lift the rod. The advantage of the rod is that a small movement of the fisherman's arm makes a large movement at the end of the rod. So a flick of the wrist casts the line which floats far across the water.

FACT BOX

• The longer a lever arm, the greater the force. Using a lever (it would have to be a strong lever) 30 feet long, with a pivot 4 inches from the end, you could lift an elephant with one finger!

• A piano is full of levers. Each key is a lever with other levers attached to it. When you press a key, the levers make hammers fly at the strings.

Body levers

The lower bones in your arm form a third-class lever with the pivot at your elbow. The muscle at the front of your upper arm is called the biceps. It makes the effort to lift a weight in your hand, which is the load.

Your arm makes a third-class lever. As it lifts up an object, the effort is between the pivot and the load.

effort · load · pivot

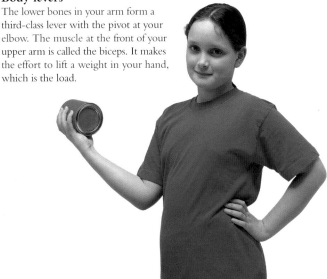

MAKING LEVERS WORK

MAKE A GRIPPER

You will need: short pencil, two pieces of wood each about 6 inches long, thick rubber bands, objects to pick up or crush such as candy or grapes.

Y ou can find out how to make two different lever machines in the projects here. The first is a simple gripper for picking up or crushing objects. It can act both as a pair of nutcrackers (a second-class lever) or a pair of tweezers (a third-class lever). In a pair of nutcrackers, the load (in this case a piece of candy) is between the pivot (the pencil) and the effort (where you push). In a pair of tweezers, the effort is between the pivot and the load. Draw a lever diagram that shows both ways of using lever machines to help you understand how each one works.

The second machine is a balance scale. It is like the ones used by the Romans about 2,000 years ago. It works by balancing the weight of an object against a known weight, in this case a bag of coins. The coins are moved along the lever arm until they balance the object being weighed. The further away from the pivot the weighted bag is, the greater turning effect it has on the lever arm. The heavier the weight being measured, the further the bag must be moved to balance the arm. The weight is read off from the scale along the arm.

1 Put the pencil between the two pieces of wood, near one end. Wrap the rubber bands tightly around the pieces of wood to make a pivot. You have now made the gripper.

2 Hold the gripper near the pivot to make it act like a pair of tweezers. See if you can pick up a delicate object, such as a piece of candy or a grape, without crushing the object.

3 Holding the gripper at the other end makes a pair of nutcrackers. It increases the force you make. Try using the nutcrackers to crack a small nut or to crush a small sweet.

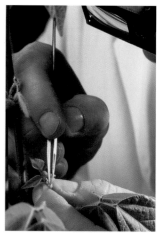

Gently does it
A pair of tweezers is used to pick up minute grains of pollen. Tweezers make it easier to pick up tiny or delicate objects. The tweezers act as a third-class lever, so the force that squeezes the object is smaller than the effort you use.

MAKE A BALANCE SCALE

You will need: thick cardboard about 20 inches x 3 inches, thin card stock, scissors, string, ruler, hole punch, 5-inch circle of cardboard, tape, 3.2 ounces of coins, felt-tipped pen, objects to weigh.

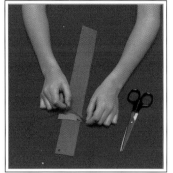

1 Make the arm by folding the thick cardboard in two. Make a loop of thin card stock and attach it to the arm so that its center is 4½ inches from one end. Tie a piece of string to this support.

2 Make a hole ½ inch from the arm's end. Make the cardboard circle into a cone-shaped pan and tie it to the hole. Make an envelope and tie it to a loop so that it hangs over the arm.

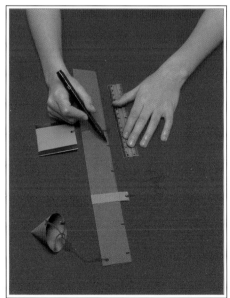

4 To weigh an object, put it in the pan and slide the envelope of coins backward and forward along the arm until the arm balances. In this picture, the arm balances when the envelope of coins reaches the third mark. The object being weighed is about 2½ ounces because each mark equals 1½ ounces.

3 Put the 3.2 ounces of coins in the envelope and seal it up. Starting from the center of the support, make a mark every 2 inches along the arm. This scale will enable you to figure out the weight of any object you put in the pan because each mark equals 1½ ounces.

WHEELS AND AXLES

Pedal pusher
Pushing on the pedals of this child's tricycle turns the axle and drives the tricycle's front wheel.

The wheel is one of the most important inventions ever made. About 6,000 years ago, people discovered that using logs as rollers was a more efficient way to move heavy loads than to drag them. A slice from a log was the first wheel. Then people found that they could attach a wheel to the end of a pole. The pole became an axle.

A wheel on the end of an axle makes a simple machine. Turning the wheel makes the axle turn, too. It is a machine because turning the axle is easier using the wheel than turning the axle on its own. Wheels and axles increase mechanical advantage—turning the wheel makes the axle turn with greater force. The bigger the wheel compared to the size of the axle, the greater the force, making turning even easier. Wheels are used in millions of machines. One of the most obvious is in wheeled vehicles, which were in use more than 4,000 years ago and are still the most common form of transport today. Sometimes wheel and axle machines can be difficult to recognize. Can you find a wheel and axle in a spanner or a door key?

handle
spindle

Winding up
The key of a wind-up toy has a handle that acts as a wheel and a spindle that is an axle. The large handle makes it easier to turn the spindle.

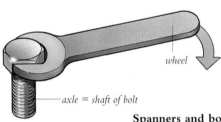

wheel
axle = shaft of bolt

Spanners and bolts
A spanner and a bolt make up a wheel and axle system. The threaded shaft of the bolt is the axle, and the handle of the spanner is the wheel. By turning the spanner, it is much easier to tighten or loosen the bolt.

Lock and key
A key doesn't look like a wheel and axle machine, but it is. A key has a small handle on the end, which makes it easier to turn in the lock. The handle acts as a wheel. The key's shaft is the axle.

Putting the spoke in

A cart full of grapes is pulled by oxen in this Roman mosaic, which was made about 1,700 years ago. Using wheeled carts meant oxen could pull a much heavier load than they could carry. The first cart wheels were made from slices of tree trunk. About 4,000 years ago, the Romans hollowed the wheels out and added spokes to make them lighter. Vehicles could now go faster.

Potter's wheels

A potter in India uses a wheel to cast his pots.
Casting pots was one of the first uses of the wheel. Simple potter's wheels are still used around the world. The massive wooden wheel can be turned either by foot or by hand.

Keep on spinning

The rim of this grinding wheel moves at very high speed as it sharpens tools. The wheel is very heavy, which means that it tends to keep spinning even when the tool is pressed against it.

Racing wheels

A racing car is moved along by its rear wheels (which are called the driving wheels). Each driving wheel is turned by an axle called a driveshaft. In most cars the driving wheels are the front wheels.

Driving in a screw

A screwdriver is a machine. Its shaft is an axle and its handle is a wheel. The handle increases the force on the shaft when it is turned to drive in a screw.

Steering wheels

A car's steering wheel is attached to the end of an axle, called the steering column. The wheel increases the force from the driver's hands, giving the driver enough force to control the car.

WHEELS AT WORK

MAKE A CAPSTAN WHEEL

You will need: pencil, small cardboard box such as a shoe box, ruler, cardboard tube, scissors, dowel, tape, string, a weight, thin card stock, glue, thick cardboard.

There are hundreds of different examples of wheels and axles. Some are very old designs, such as the capstan wheel. A capstan is a wheel on an axle with handles that stretch out from the edge of the wheel. The handles are used to turn the wheel, which turns the axle. Large capstan wheels can be turned by animals as they walk around and around, or by several people who each push on a handle. In the past, they were a familiar sight on ships and in dockyards, where they were used to raise heavy loads such as a ship's anchor. This project shows you how to make a simple capstan wheel for lifting a weight. At the end of the project, a ratchet is attached to the axle. A ratchet is a very useful device that acts like a catch. It prevents the capstan wheel from turning back on itself once you have stopped winding it.

1 Draw a line around the box about one-third from the top. Place the tube on the line, draw around it and cut out a circle. Repeat on the opposite side of the box, so the circles match.

2 Cut four slots in one end of the tube. Lay two pieces of dowel in the slots so that they cross over. Tape the dowel in place. You have now made the capstan wheel.

3 Push the tube into the holes in the box. Tape the end of a piece of string to the middle of the tube inside the box. Tie a heavy object to the other end of the string.

Around in circles

Sailors on board a sailing ship turn a capstan wheel. The wheel turns a drum that pulls the ship's heavy anchor up from the sea bed. The longer the handles on the capstan wheel, the easier it is to turn the drum, but the farther the sailors have to walk. Pulling up the anchor by hauling in the cable would be much more difficult.

4 Stand the box on a table edge so the weight hangs down. Turn the capstan wheel to lift the object. Try turning the handles at their ends and then near the wheel's center.

5 To make a ratchet, cut four small rectangles of cardboard and carefully glue them to the tube at the opposite end to the capstan wheel. These will form the ratchet teeth.

6 From a piece of thick cardboard, cut an L-shaped piece. Bend one of the legs of the L at a right angle to the other leg. This will form the part that locks into the ratchet teeth.

8 Wind up the capstan wheel to lift the weight again. You should now be able to let go of the capstan without the weight dropping back to the ground. The teeth will catch on the L shape, stopping the axle from turning backward.

7 Glue the cardboard L to the top of your box so that the end hanging over the edge just catches in the ratchet teeth. Let the glue dry before trying your ratchet.

Crushing the grapes

A wine press crushes grapes from a vineyard to release the grape juice that is used for wine-making. The press is operated by turning a nut at the top that forces a screw thread downward into the tub. The horizontal bar on the nut works like a capstan. Pushing in opposite directions on its ends turns the nut. The longer the bar, the greater the turning force on the nut, and the greater the force on the grapes.

SLOPING RAMPS

How can an inclined plane, or ramp, be a machine? It is a type of machine because it makes going uphill, or moving an object uphill against the force of gravity, much easier. Think about a moving van and people trying to lift a heavy box inside it. It might take two people working together to lift the box up high enough to reach into the van. One person could push the box up a gently sloping ramp on his or her own.

Ramps are useful in many different situations. You often see ramps on building sites, and stairs are ramps, too. The shallower (less steep) the slope, the easier it is to move an object up it, but the further the object must move to gain the same amount of height. For example, when you are walking uphill on a zig-zag path you are using ramps. Walking along the gently sloping sections of the path is easier than walking straight up the steep hillside, but you have to walk much further to reach the top. Railways have to use winding routes to go up hills because trains cannot get up very steep hills without sliding backward.

Mud-brick ramp
These are the remains of a ramp made of mud bricks. The ramp was built by the Ancient Egyptians about 3,000 years ago. Egyptian pyramid and temple builders had no cranes. They used ramps to move building materials up to where they were needed.

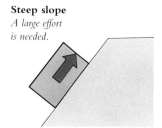

Steep slope
*A large effort
is needed.*

Shallow slope
*A small effort
is needed.*

*On a steep slope, all the
work is done in a short
distance and needs a large effort.
On a gentle slope, the work is done over
a much longer distance, making it easier.*

Ramps for building
A ramp is being used to construct a building in this picture, which was copied from an ancient Egyptian tomb painting. Without construction machines such as cranes, the Egyptians had to build huge sloping ramps to pull stone blocks to the upper levels of the building.

Ramps for loading

A car is driven up a ramp on to the back of a delivery truck. Long, gently sloping ramps are easier to drive up than short, steep ones. Loading and unloading cars from a transporter truck is easy using ramps because the cars can be driven on and off the truck. No winches or cranes are needed.

Fast track

When engineers plan roads such as highways, they try to avoid steep carriageways. Cuttings and embankments are built into hillsides to provide gentle slopes. Vehicles are able to climb the slopes without having to slow down too much.

Access ramps

A disabled man is using a ramp to get down to the beach. Ramps make it much easier for vehicles with wheels to travel from one level to another. Many public buildings, such as libraries, sports centers and hospitals, often have ramps leading up to their doors as well as steps. Without ramps, people with wheelchairs find it very difficult to get in and out of buildings.

Zigzag roads

Mountain roads, such as this one in South Africa, zigzag upward in a series of gentle slopes. A road straight up the side of the valley would be much too steep for most vehicles to drive up.

FACT BOX

• Most canals have flights of locks to move boats up and down hill, but a few use inclined planes, or ramps. In a 1-mile-long inclined plane in Belgium, the boats float inside huge 5,000-ton tanks of water. The tanks are hauled up the inclined plane on rails.

• The railway line from Lima to Galera, in Peru, climbs 14,340 feet. In some places the track zigzags backward and forward across the very steep hillsides.

WEDGES AND SCREWS

A pair of scissors and your front teeth have something in common. They are simple machines called wedges that use inclined planes (ramps) to work. A wedge is a type of ramp, or two ramps back-to-back. Pushing the thin end of a wedge into a narrow gap with a small effort makes the wedge press hard on the edges of the gap, forcing the gap apart. Chisels, axes and plows all work with wedges. If you look closely at their blades you will see that they widen from the cutting edge.

Screw threads are also a type of inclined plane. Imagine a long, narrow ramp wrapped around a pole. This is what a screw thread is. Screw threads make screws, nuts and bolts and car jacks work. It only takes a small effort to turn a screw thread to make it move in or out with great force. Screw threads provide a very secure way of attaching something together, or of raising a heavy load.

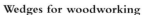

Wedging a door
A door wedge stops a door from opening or closing. Pulling on the door pulls the bottom of the door further up the wedge's ramp. This makes the wedge press even harder against the bottom of the door and the floor.

Wedges as cutters
An axe is used to cut down a tree. The axe head is wedge-shaped. When it hits the wood, its sharp edge sinks in, forcing the wood apart and splitting it. The handle allows the person operating the axe to swing it with great speed and lever out pieces of wood.

Wedges for woodworking
Wedges are useful for shaping materials. The axe in the foreground uses a wedge to split wood. The woodworker in the background is using a small wedge-shaped tool to remove small amounts of material from the wood, which is spun at high speed by a foot pedal.

Digging with screws
The screw-shaped tool in this picture is called an auger. It is used to dig deep holes for fence posts, or for filling with concrete, to make secure foundations for buildings. The auger is operated by a mechanical digger. The auger both loosens soil from the bottom of the hole and transports the soil to the surface.

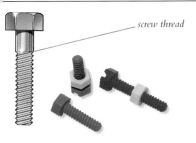

screw thread

Screws

A screw uses a screw thread to attach itself firmly into wood or metal. A screw thread is a ramp wrapped around a pole. Turning the thread is like moving up or down the slope.

bolt

nut

Nuts and bolts

A nut and bolt are used to join objects together. The screw threads on the nut and bolt interlock so that turning the nut makes it move down the bolt.

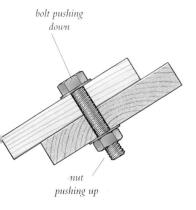

bolt pushing down

nut pushing up

When the nut is screwed onto the bolt the combined force of the nut and bolt squeezes the two pieces of wood tightly together.

Spiraling slope

A corkscrew has a screw thread that makes it wind into a cork as the handle is turned. The screw only moves a small way into the cork for each turn of the handle. This makes winding the corkscrew quite easy.

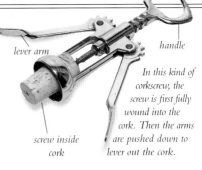

lever arm

handle

screw inside cork

In this kind of corkscrew, the screw is first fully wound into the cork. Then the arms are pushed down to lever out the cork.

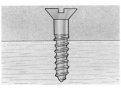

Uncorking a bottle

A corkscrew such as this one combines three simple machines: the wheel and axle, the wedge and the lever. The handle of the corkscrew acts as a capstan to make turning in the screw easier. One end then folds down to rest on top the bottle's neck, and the other end forms a lever for pulling out the cork.

The point of a wood screw helps it to sink into the wood. The thread makes the point go in deeper as the screw is turned.

Driving force

Using a screwdriver increases the force with which you can turn a screw. As it turns, the screw thread bites into the wood. The screw is also wedge-shaped to help it force its way into the wood. Using screws is a strong and secure way of attaching all kinds of materials together.

PLANES AT WORK

Although screw threads are most commonly used for joining things together, they can also be used to lift a weight upward. In a screw jack, the force made by turning the screw thread is used to lift a weight upward. With a screw jack, a huge weight, such as a car, can be lifted easily, but slowly. One turn on the handle of the jack using a small effort raises the heavy load a tiny bit.

The first project on these pages shows you how to make a simple type of screw jack. The second project shows you how to make a device to measure force, or the effort needed to raise an object. Use it to compare how a gentler slope makes lifting an object easier.

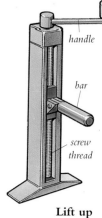

handle

bar

screw
thread

Lift up
If a tire gets punctured, the driver can lift the car with a screw jack before changing the tire. The driver places the jack on the ground with the bar underneath the car. As the driver turns the handle, the bar moves up the screw thread and lifts the car.

MAKE A SCREW JACK

You will need: *piece of wooden board or thick cardboard, long bolt with two nuts and washers to fit, strong glue, popsicle stick or short piece of wood, cardboard tube, cardboard, a weight to lift.*

Squashing with screws
The apple press uses a screw to squeeze the juice from apples. Turning the screw is quite easy, but it makes a huge force for crushing the apples.

1 Put a nut on one end of the bolt. Glue the bolt to the middle of a square piece of wooden board or thick cardboard so that the thread is pointing upward. Let dry.

2 Glue the end of the popsicle stick to the side of a nut (the nut must fit the bolt) to make a handle. When the glue is dry, wind the nut onto the bolt and put the washer on top.

3 Stick the tube to a cardboard rectangle. Place the tube over the bolt so it rests on top of the washer. Move a weight up and down by turning the handle on the nut.

MAKE A FORCE MEASURER

You will need: piece of wood or thick cardboard, rubber band, paper fastener, string, pencil or felt-tipped pen, ruler, model vehicle, materials to make a slope (such as a plank and books).

1 Measure and cut a piece of wood or cardboard about 6 inches x 2 inches. Attach the rubber band near one end with a paper fastener. Tie a piece of string to the other end of the band.

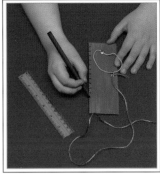

2 Mark inches along one edge of the wood, for recording how far the rubber band stretches when it is pulled by the weight. You have now made your force measurer.

3 Use your force measurer to find the weight of the model vehicle. Hang the model from your measurer and note where the band stretches to. Write down the measurement.

On a level

The Ancient Egyptians used ramps to lift huge stone blocks to build their pyramids. As the building progressed, more ramps were added so that they were always level with the top of the building.

4 Make a slope—try using a plank propped up on books. How much force is needed to pull the vehicle up the slope? Is it more or less than the model's weight? Try again with a shallower slope. Does the force needed change? You should see that it needs less force to pull the model vehicle up the shallower slope.

LIFTING WITH PULLEYS

Using a pulley is often the easiest way to lift a heavy load high up. The pulley is a simple machine. The most basic pulley system is a wheel with a groove in its rim in which a rope is placed. The wheel rotates around an axle. The rope hangs down on either side of the wheel, with one end attached to a load. Pulling down on the rope lifts the load hanging on the other end. It does not reduce the amount of force needed to lift an object, so there is no mechanical advantage. It does, however, make lifting the load easier, because it is easier to pull down than it is to pull up. A pulley's special advantage is that it changes the direction of the force.

Using several pulleys together makes lifting even easier, and many pulley systems have more than one wheel that operate together. A pulley system such as this is called a block and tackle. Pulleys are useful for lifting loads on building sites and dockyards, and for moving heavy parts and machinery in factories.

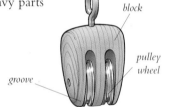

block

pulley wheel

groove

A block and tackle has two blocks like the one shown above, arranged one above the other. The pulley wheels are designed to turn easily as the rope runs around them, through the groove.

Pulling down
The simplest pulley system is a single pulley wheel with a rope running over it. It changes the direction of the pull (the effort) needed to lift an object (the load) off the ground. Instead of pulling up on the object, the boy is pulling down on the rope. He can use his weight to help.

Winching with pulleys
An air-sea rescue helicopter uses a an electric winch to lift sailors from the sea on the end of a wire. The wire runs from the winch over a pulleywheel on the side of the helicopter.

Pulleys for building
Workmen use a pulley to lift building materials to construct the walls of a great city in the 1500s. The workman at the bottom turns a handle to haul up the bucket. The pulley was probably devised by Ancient Greeks about 2,500 years ago and has been in use ever since.

Half the effort

This pulley system has two pulley wheels. Pulling the rope raises the lower wheel and the load. With two wheels, the effort needed to lift the load is halved. This makes it easier, but the rope has to be pulled twice as far.

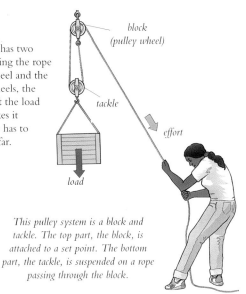

block (pulley wheel)

tackle

effort

load

This pulley system is a block and tackle. The top part, the block, is attached to a set point. The bottom part, the tackle, is suspended on a rope passing through the block.

Up and away

A light pull on the loop of chain lifts a very heavy boat engine. This pulley system has a very high mechanical advantage—it takes little effort to pull a massive weight.

Dockyard block and tackle

The lower end of the block and tackle on a dockyard crane can be seen in this picture. The crane is lifting heavy pallets of cargo from the deep hold of a ship.

Boats away!

A ship's lifeboats hang on pulley systems ready to be lowered quickly into the sea if the ship has to be abandoned. The pulley systems allow the heavy boats to be lowered by one person standing inside the boat itself.

Higher and higher

A dockyard crane uses pulley systems to lift very heavy loads. The cable from the pulley is winched in and out by an engine to make the lifting hook rise and fall. Other engines move the crane's arm up and down.

PULLEYS AT WORK

The two projects on these pages illustrate how pulley systems work. In the first project, a simple double pulley system is constructed. It does not have pulley wheels. Instead, the string passes over smooth metal hoops. This would be no good for a real system because friction between the rope and metal would be too great, but it does show how a pulley system is connected together.

The second project investigates how adding more turns on a block and tackle reduces the effort needed to move a load. You may notice, however, that the more turns you make, the greater the friction becomes. Using wheels in a block and tackle cuts down on this friction.

Lifting materials
A pulley is useful for lifting materials up to a new building's upper floors. It does not increase the lifting power here, but works because it is easier to pull down on a rope than up.

Linking up
Heavy-duty block and tackle systems, like this one in a dockyard, are used for lifting the heavy cargo. They have metal chain links, which are much stronger than a rope would be. The chain links interlock with the shaped pulley wheels.

MAKE A SIMPLE PULLEY

You will need:
lengths of string,
two large paperclips,
a weight.

1 Take a short length of string. Use the string to tie a large paperclip to a door handle, or coat hook on a wall. Make sure the paperclip is tied securely to its support.

2 Cut a long piece of string and feed it through the paperclip's inner hoop. Now feed it through the top of a second paperclip and tie it to the outer hoop of the top clip.

3 Tie a weight, using another piece of string, to the bottom paperclip. Pull the end of the long string to lift the bottom paperclip, which will lift the weight.

MAKE A BLOCK AND TACKLE

You will need:
*two broom handles or
lengths of thick dowel,
strong string or thin rope,
two friends.*

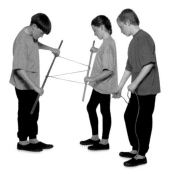

1 Ask each of your friends to hold a broom handle, or length of dowel, between outstretched hands. Tie the end of a long piece of string, or rope, to one handle.

2 Wrap the string around each handle once, keeping the loops fairly close together on the handles. Now pull on the string. How easy was it to pull your friends together?

FACT BOX

• Using a block-and-tackle system with a mechanical advantage of 20 (with ten wheels at each end), you could lift an elephant easily by hand!

• One of the first people to make use of block and tackle systems was the famous Greek scientist Archimedes. He is said to have pulled ships ashore with them, in the third century B.C.

3 Now wrap the string twice around each handle, making sure you keep the turns close together. Now pull on the end of the string again. What differences do you notice this time? Is it any easier?

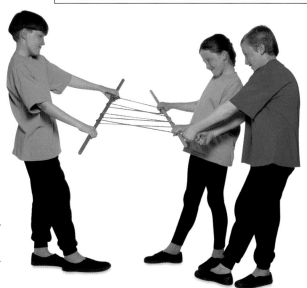

4 Make more turns around the handles and try pulling again. Do more turns make the effort you need to make smaller? Do you have to pull the rope farther than before?

GEAR WHEELS

A gear is a wheel with teeth around its edge. When two gear wheels are put next to each other, their teeth can be made to interlock. Then when one wheel turns, the other one turns, too. Gears are used to transmit movement from one wheel to another. If both wheels are the same size, the wheels turn at the same speed. If one wheel is bigger than the other, the gears can be used to speed up or slow down movement, or to increase or decrease a force. Many machines, from kitchen whisks to trucks, have gears that help them to work.

Belt drives and chain drives are similar to gears. In these, two wheels are linked together by a belt or a chain instead of teeth. This is another way of transferring power and movement from one wheel to another. Speed can also be varied by changing the size of the wheels.

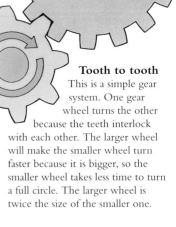

Tooth to tooth
This is a simple gear system. One gear wheel turns the other because the teeth interlock with each other. The larger wheel will make the smaller wheel turn faster because it is bigger, so the smaller wheel takes less time to turn a full circle. The larger wheel is twice the size of the smaller one.

Mining with gears
Huge gear wheels are part of an old lift mechanism from a mine. The teeth on the interlocking gear wheels press very hard against each other. They need to be very wide and thick so that they don't snap off.

Transmitting a force
In the center of this kitchen whisk is a set of gears. They are used to transmit the turning movement of the handle to the blades of the whisk. The gears speed up the movement, making the blades spin faster than the turning handle. The gears turn the movement through a right angle, too. These sort of gears are called bevelled gears.

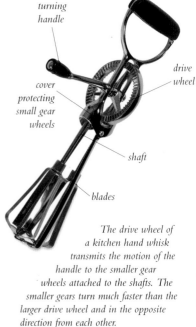

turning handle

cover protecting small gear wheels

drive wheel

shaft

blades

The drive wheel of a kitchen hand whisk transmits the motion of the handle to the smaller gear wheels attached to the shafts. The smaller gears turn much faster than the larger drive wheel and in the opposite direction from each other.

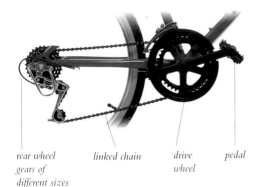

All geared up

Bicycle gears use wheels and a chain to transmit the drive from the pedals to the bicycle's rear wheel. As a rider turns the pedals, the drive wheel is moved around. This moves a linked chain, which turns a set of gear wheels of different sizes attached to the rear wheel. With the chain on the largest of these gears (in low gear), pedaling is easy but the bicycle travels slowly. With the chain on the smallest gear (in high gear), pedaling is harder but the bicycle moves faster.

rear wheel   *linked chain*   *drive*   *pedal*
gears of   *wheel*
different sizes

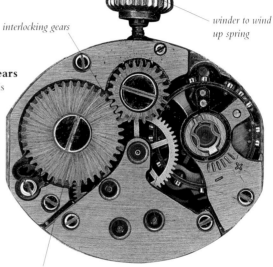

interlocking gears

winder to wind
up spring

Wind-up watch gears

The back has been removed from this wind-up watch so you can see the tiny gear wheels inside. Different-sized gear wheels are arranged so that they move the hands of the watch at different speeds. The clock is powered by a spring, wound up by hand. The spring makes a gear wheel turn, which moves the minute hand. Another gear slows down this movement to turn the hour hand.

gears transmit
energy from spring

Swinging time keeper

This pendulum clock uses gear wheels to control its speed. A spring drives one gear around, which drives other gears that show time. The speed that gears turn at is controlled by a swinging pendulum that interlocks with the teeth on a gear wheel called the escape wheel. The escape wheel gives the pendulum a small push on each swing to keep the pendulum moving.

Belt drives

Wide belts, called belt drives, stretch between wheels in the roof and the machines of a factory. The photograph was taken in about 1905. The wheels in the roof are turned by an engine, and the belts transmit this movement to drive the machines.

MAKING GEARS WORK

Before engineers used metals, they made gear wheels from wood. One way of making gear-wheel teeth was to attach short poles to the edge of a thick disc. The poles on different gear wheels interlocked to transmit movement. Gears like this were being used 2,000 years ago. If you visit an old mill, you might still see similar wooden gears today. The first project shows you how to make a simple gear wheel system. What do you notice about how the wheels turn? They turn in different directions and the smaller wheel (with fewer teeth) turns one and a half times for every one rotation of the larger wheel. The second project shows you how to make a simple belt drive and how it can turn an axle at different speeds.

Slow pedal power
Old sewing machines, such as this one, were powered by a foot pedal that turned a large pulley wheel. This wheel was linked by a drive belt to a small pulley wheel on the machine. So pedaling slowly made the small wheel turn quickly.

MAKE A SET OF GEAR WHEELS

You will need: compass and pencil, protractor, thick cardboard, scissors, used matchsticks or thin dowel, glue, paper fasteners, small cardboard box.

Spiral gears
A computer graphic image shows part of a car gear box. These gears are helical (spiral) gears, which are more efficient than gears with straight teeth.

3 Use paper fasteners to attach one wheel to the top of the box and the other to the side so that the teeth interlock. Turn one disc to turn the other.

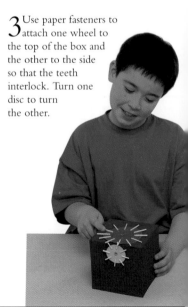

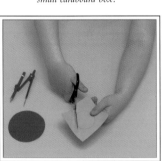

1 Using a pencil and a compass, mark out two discs on cardboard and cut them out. Make the diameter of one disc twice the diameter of the other, for example 3 inches and 1½ inches.

2 Glue eight matches around the edge of the small disc. First glue four matches in a cross shape, then add four more half-way. In a similar way, glue 12 matches to the large disc.

MAKE A BELT DRIVE

You will need: cardboard box, dowel, scissors, strips of thin card stock, glue, thick rubber band, felt-tipped pen.

1 Cut two pieces of dowel each about 2 inches longer than the width of the box. Cut two holes in both sides of the box. Slide the rods through to make two axles.

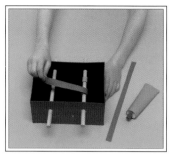

2 Cut a strip of card stock. Glue it to one of the axles. Wrap it round and glue the end down to make a wheel. Make a bigger wheel with a strip of card stock three times longer than the first.

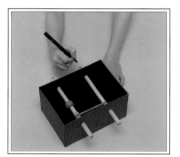

3 Put a wide rubber band around both axles. The band should be slightly stretched when it is in place. Make a mark at the end of each axle so you can see how fast they turn.

Printing gear

Computer printers use gears driven by electric motors to move sheets of paper past the print head (where the ink is fired onto the paper) bit by bit at the correct speed. More gears move the print head from side to side, making up lines of the image.

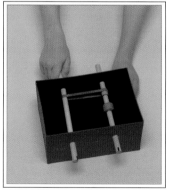

4 To test your belt drive, put the rubber band onto the smaller wheel and start turning the plain axle. Does the wheeled axle turn more or fewer times than the plain?

5 Now move the rubber band onto the larger wheel and start turning the plain axle again. What difference does it make to the speed of the wheeled axle? Use the pen marks to compare the speeds.

POWER FOR MACHINES

Early machines, such as axes and ramps, relied on human muscle power to make them work. Then people started using animals to work many simple machines. Animals, such as oxen, can carry, pull and lift much heavier loads than people can. Eventually people realized they could capture the energy of the wind or flowing water by using windmills and water-wheels. These became the first machines to create power that in turn was used to make other machines work. This energy was used to do such things as grinding grain to make flour or pumping up water from underground.

Today, wind and water energy are still captured to generate electricity, which we use to light and power our homes, schools, offices and factories.

Wind for milling

A windmill uses the power of the wind to turn heavy mill stones that grind grain to make flour. The whole building can be turned around so that the sails are facing into the wind. The speed of the mill is controlled by opening and closing slots in the sails.

Power walking

A man is operating a treadmill in Australia in the 1840s. He is walking up the rungs so that his weight turns the wheel. The movement of the wheel is used to operate machinery. Human treadmills are no longer used.

Overshot water-wheel

There are two different types of water-wheel. This one is called an overshot wheel because the water flows over the top of the wheel and falls into buckets on the wheel. The water's weight pulls the wheel around.

Undershot water-wheel

The second type of water-wheel is called an undershot wheel because rushing water in a stream or river flows under the wheel and catches in the buckets at the bottom of the wheel. The force of the water spins the wheel.

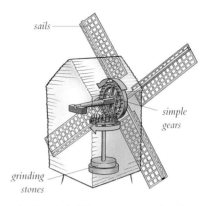

sails

simple gears

grinding stones

Grinding stones
Many windmills and watermills generate power to turn millstones. The grinding stones in this picture are used to squeeze oil from olives. Only the top millstone turns while the bottom stone stays still.

Inside a windmill is an arrangement of wooden gear wheels, which transfers power from the sails to the grinding stones. Mills like this have been in use for centuries.

Modern mills
Wind turbines, like these shown on a wind farm, are a modern type of windmill. The wind spins the huge propellers, which turn an electricity generator inside the top of each turbine.

Power from water
A hydroelectric station generates electricity from the water of a fast-flowing river. The water is stored behind a huge dam. As it flows out, it spins a turbine, which is like a very efficient water-wheel. The turbine turns a generator, which makes electricity.

Underground power
In the underground turbine hall of a hydroelectric power station, each of the generators can produce about a gigawatt of electricity—enough electricity to work about 10 million light bulbs.

WIND AND WATER POWER

Modern windmills are called wind turbines and are used to generate electricity. The most efficient wind turbines only have two or three blades, as in the propeller of an aircraft. Hundreds of wind turbines can be grouped together to make a wind farm. Sometimes one or two large turbines generate enough electricity to power a small community. There are several shapes of wind turbine. One of the most efficient is the vertical–axis type. This has an axle standing vertical to the ground. It is very efficient because it works no matter which way the wind is blowing.

   The first project shows you how to make a vertical–axis turbine. The second project shows you how to make an overshot water–wheel. This captures the energy of falling water to lift a small weight. Try pouring the water onto the wheel from different heights to see if it makes a difference to the wheel's speed.

MAKE A WINDMILL

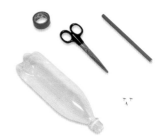

You will need:
plastic bottle, scissors, tape, thin dowel, tacks.

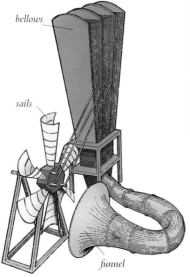

bellows

sails

funnel

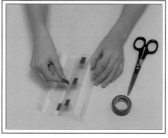

1 Cut the top and bottom off the bottle to leave a tube. Cut the tube in half lengthwise, then stick the two halves together in an S shape, so the edges overlap by 1 inch.

2 The piece of dowel should be about 1½ inches longer than the vanes. Slide it into the slot between the vanes. Press a tack gently into each end of the dowel.

Round and round again
This machine was devised in the 1500s by an Italian inventor. He believed that as the sails turned, they would operate a set of bellows. The bellows in turn would provide enough wind to drive the sails to set up a continuous cycle of movement. It cannot work because the sails do not provide enough energy to squeeze the bellows.

3 To make the windmill spin, hold it vertically with your fingers on the tacks at each end of the dowel. Blow on the vanes. The windmill will spin easily.

MAKE A WATER-WHEEL

You will need: large plastic bottle, scissors, wire (ask an adult to cut the bottom out of a coat hanger), cork, craft knife, tape, string, weight, pitcher of water, large plate.

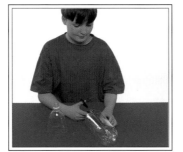

1 Cut the top third off the plastic bottle. Cut a small hole in the bottom piece near the base (this is to let the water out). Cut a V-shape on each side of the rim.

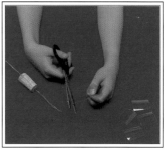

2 Ask an adult to push the wire through the center of the cork to make an axle. From the top third of the plastic bottle, cut six small curved vanes as shown.

3 Ask an adult to cut six slots in the cork with a craft knife. (This might be easier without the wire.) Push the plastic vanes into the slots to make the water-wheel.

4 Rest the wheel's axle in the V-shaped slots. Tape a length of string toward one end of the axle and tie a small weight to the end of the string. Fill a pitcher with water.

FACT BOX

• In a strong breeze, the world's largest wind turbine, in Hawaii, would be capable of operating more than 4,000 microwave ovens.

• China's Three Gorges Dam will generate 18 gigawatts of electricity—enough to power 24 million microwave ovens!

5 Put the water-wheel on a large plate or in the sink. Pour water onto the wheel so that it hits the upward-curving vanes. The weight should be lifted.

Animal power

A water-raising wheel such as this one would be operated by an animal or a person walking in a circle, pulling the horizontal pole on the right. Buckets attached to a chain driven by the wheel go down into the well, scoop up water, lift it, and empty it into a chute.

ENGINES AND MOTORS

Many modern machines are powered by engines and motors, which are complicated machines themselves. An engine is a machine that makes movement energy from heat. The heat is made by burning a fuel, such as gas. The first engines were driven by steam.

Most engines today, such as the ones used in cars, are internal combustion engines. This means that the fuel is burned inside the engine. In a car engine, as the gas explodes, it produces hot gases that push pistons inside cylinders up and down. The pistons turn a crankshaft, which carries the movement energy from the engine to the wheels of the car. An electric motor is a machine that makes movement energy from electricity rather than from burning fuel. Most of the electricity we use is made in power stations or from the chemicals inside batteries.

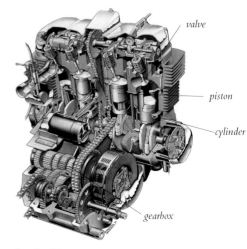

valve

piston

cylinder

gearbox

Burning inside
This diagram shows the pistons inside the internal combustion engine of a car. At the top are valves that let fuel and air into the pistons and let exhaust gases out. At the bottom is the gearbox that sends the power from the engine to the wheels.

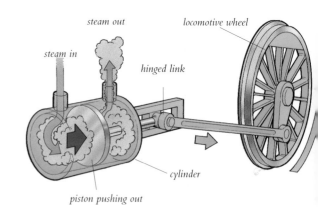

steam out

locomotive wheel

steam in

hinged link

cylinder

piston pushing out

Early steam power
An atmospheric engine was one of the first types of steam engines. Steam was fed to a cylinder, where it was cooled and turned back to water, forming a vacuum. The atmospheric pressure outside the cylinder pushed the piston in.

Piston power
In a steam engine, steam made by heating water in a boiler is forced along a pipe into a cylinder. The pressure of the steam pushes a piston in the cylinder outward. The moving piston then turns a wheel that is used to drive a locomotive or power a machine.

Engines for cars

A car's internal combustion engine is usually fitted under the hood. The engine's cylinders are inside the large black engine block. You can see the exhaust pipes that carry waste gases away from the cylinders.

Under the hood

The top of an internal combustion engine in a small truck. On the left are the starter motor (an electric motor that makes the engine turn to start it up) and the alternator, that makes electricity for the electrical parts, such as the lights, of the truck.

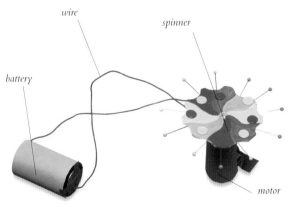

Electric motors

Electricity is turned into movement by an electric motor. When the motor is connected to a battery, its shaft spins around. Electric motors are small and clean, which makes them useful for household gadgets.

wire

spinner

battery

motor

An electric motor with a colorful spinner on top is connected to a battery by two wires. This makes an electric circuit.

HYDRAULICS AND PNEUMATICS

Did you know that a machine can be powered by a liquid or a gas? Machines that have parts moved by a liquid are called hydraulic machines. Those that have parts moved by a gas are called pneumatic machines. A simple hydraulic system has a pipe filled with oil and a piston (a cylinder that moves back and forth) at each end. Pushing one piston into the pipe forces the piston at the other end outward, transmitting power from one end of the pipe to the other. In a simple pneumatic system, compressed air is used to force a piston to move.

Hydraulic and pneumatic machines can be very powerful. They are also quite simple and very robust. Machines that work in dirty and rough conditions, such as diggers, drills and dump trucks, often have hydraulic or pneumatic systems instead of motors. Most dental drills are also worked by a pneumatic system. Air, pumped to the drill, makes a tiny turbine inside the drill spin very fast.

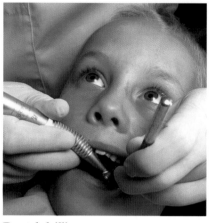

Dental drilling
The high-pitched whine of a dental drill is made by the air that powers it. Inside is an air turbine that spins an amazing 10,000 times a second as air is pumped through it.

Pump it up
Using an air pump is a simple way to blow up a balloon. A valve in the pump's outlet allows air to be pumped into the balloon as the piston is pushed in. It prevents the air from being sucked out again when the piston is pulled out.

Lift it up
Pneumatic power can lift a book. The girl blows air into the inflated balloon and pushes the book upward. Less effort is needed to lift the book like this than is needed to lift it by hand.

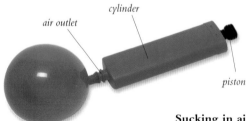

air outlet

cylinder

piston

Sucking in air
All pneumatic machines need a device to suck in air from the outside and push it into the machine. This is called an air pump, or a compressor. The simple air pump above sucks in air as the piston is pulled back, and forces air out as the piston is pushed in.

Hydraulic lift

Lifting and moving a heavy load is made easy with a hydraulically-powered machine such as a fork-lift truck. The forks are lifted by hydraulic rams. Each ram consists of a cylinder and a piston that moves inside it. Pumping special oil, called hydraulic fluid, into the cylinder makes the piston move in or out, depending on which end of the cylinder the oil is pumped into.

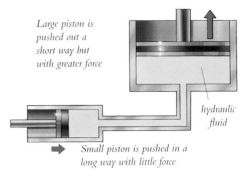

Large piston is pushed out a short way but with greater force

hydraulic fluid

Small piston is pushed in a long way with little force

Pushing in, pushing out

A simple hydraulic system has two pistons connected by a cylinder filled with hydraulic fluid. Using different-sized pistons creates a mechanical advantage. Pushing the small piston creates a greater force at the large one.

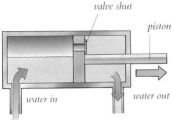

valve shut

piston

water in

water out

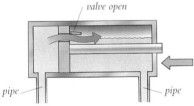

valve open

pipe

pipe

Hydraulic digging

The sections of the arm of a digger are moved by powerful hydraulic rams, each with a cylinder and piston. Hydraulic fluid is pumped to the cylinders by a pump powered by the digger's diesel engine. The fluid flows along very strong pipes called hydraulic lines, which you can see on the upper part of the arm.

Pumping water

Moving a water pump's piston in and out moves water from the pipe on the left to the pipe on the right. The valve opens to let water through as the piston moves in. The valve shuts automatically as the piston moves out because the water presses the valve closed.

Breaking through

A pneumatic drill is an air-powered drill used to break up road surfaces and concrete. The air forces the drill's heavy blade to jump up and down very quickly. The drill needs a supply of compressed air to make it work, which comes along a strong, rubber pipe from a machine called a compressor.

LIQUID AND AIR AT WORK

MAKE AN HYDRAULIC LIFTER

You will need: large plastic bottle, scissors, airtight plastic bag, plastic tubing, tape, plastic funnel, spray can lid, heavy weight, pitcher of water.

Hydraulic machinery uses a liquid to transmit power, while pneumatic machinery uses compressed air. The first project shows you how to make a simple hydraulic machine that uses water pressure to lift an object upward. A central reservoir (a pitcher of water) is poured into a pipe. The water fills up a plastic bag, which is forced to expand in a narrow cylinder. This forces up a platform, which in turn raises a heavy object. Many cranes, excavators and trucks use this principle to lift heavy loads, using hydraulic rams.

The second project shows you how to make a simple air pump. An air pump works by sucking air in one hole and pushing it out of another. A valve stops the air from being sucked in and pushed out of the wrong holes. When the air tries to flow through one way, the valve opens, but when the air tries to flow through the other way the valve stays shut.

1 Cut the top off the large plastic bottle. Make sure the plastic bag is airtight and wrap its neck over the end of a length of plastic tubing. Seal the bag to the tube with tape.

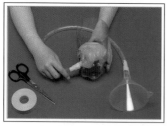

2 Attach a funnel to the other end of the tube. Make a hole at the base of the bottle and feed the bag and tubing through. The bag should sit in the bottom of the bottle.

Firing water
Fire-fighters spray water on to fires through hoses so that they can stand back from the flames. The water is pumped along the hoses by a powerful pump on the fire engine.

3 Put the spray can lid on top of the bag and rest a book, or another heavy object, on top of the bottle. Lift the funnel end of the tubing up, and slowly pour in water. What happens to the can lid and the book?

MAKE AN AIR PUMP

You will need: large plastic bottle, scissors, hammer, small nails, wooden stick or dowel, cardboard, tape, ping-pong ball.

1 Cut around the large plastic bottle, about one third up from the bottom. Cut a slit down the side of the bottom part of the bottle so that it will slide inside the top part.

2 Ask an adult to help you nail the bottom of the bottle to the end of a wooden stick or piece of dowel. You have now made a piston for your air pump.

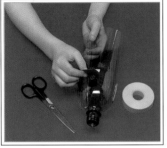

3 Cut a hole about ½ inch across near the neck of the bottle. Cut a piece of cardboard about 1 inch x 1 inch. Tape one edge of the cardboard to the bottle to form a flap over the hole.

4 Drop a ping-pong ball into the top part of the bottle so that it rests in the neck. Push the bottom part of the bottle (the piston) into the top part (the cylinder).

FACT BOX

• A fire-engine pump can pump 1,000 quarts of water a minute—enough to fill eight large soda bottles a second.

• Fire-fighters free people trapped in crashed cars with hydraulically powered cutting and spreading machines.

Skip-lifting truck
A skip truck has hydraulic rams to lift a full skip. The rams are controlled by levers near the cab, and powered by a pump operated by the engine.

5 Move the piston in and out to suck air into the bottle and out of the hole. Can you see how both the valves work? The flap should automatically close when you pull the piston out.

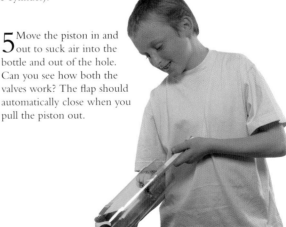

MACHINES AT HOME

Your home is full of machines. Look in the kitchen, the bathroom, the living room and bedroom. In your kitchen you should find several simple gadgets, such as can-openers, taps, scissors and bottle openers. There might also be more complicated machines, such as a washing machine or a dishwasher. Other machines you might find include a vacuum cleaner and a refrigerator. In other rooms there may be a hairdryer, a shower and a television. Even the zippers on your clothes are machines. Think about how each one saves you time and effort. What would life be like without them?

Most machines not only save you work, but also improve the results—a modern washing machine cleans clothes better than an old-fashioned tub, and a vacuum cleaner is more efficient than a broom. Many machines save time, too. For example, it is much quicker to heat food in a microwave oven than over an open fire. Many of these machines need electricity to work and are powered from the mains supply.

zipper

Zip it up
One of the simplest machines is the zipper. If you look carefully at a zipper fastener, you will see a wedge shape in the middle. This forces the two edges of the zipper together to do it up, and apart again to undo it. Before there were zippers, people had to fasten their clothes with buttons or hooks and eyes, which took longer.

lever arm

wheel and axle

wedge

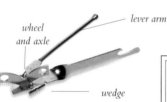

Can-opener
Can you see four different types of machine in a can opener? You should be able to find levers, a wedge, a wheel and axle and a gear wheel. Together, they make it simple to open a can.

FACT BOX

• The zipper was invented in 1893. The first zippers were unreliable, until tiny bumps and hollows were added to the end of each tooth, to help the teeth interlock.

• Electrically powered domestic machines were only possible once mains electricity was developed in the 1880s.

• One of the earliest vacuum cleaners was built in England, in 1901. It was so large that it had to be pulled by a horse and powered by a gas engine!

• The spin dryer was conceived of by a French engineer in 1865, but it was not developed until the 1920s.

What, no bag?

This clever bagless cleaner spins the dusty air at high speed, which throws the dust to the sides of the dust-collecting container. Most vacuum cleaners have a bag that lets air through but traps dust, and the bag has to be replaced regularly. The bagless cleaner's container lasts for much longer.

How a refrigerator works

Inside a refrigerator is a pump that squeezes a special liquid called a refrigerant. As the refrigerant expands again, it uses up heat, making the compartment cold.

Washing by machine

A modern washing machine is a combination of several machines. It has electric motors (to turn the drum), pumps (to pump water in and out) and valves (that let water in or out). All these machines are controlled by an automatic programme timer.

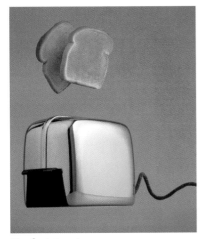

Hairdryer

Small, mains-powered electric motors make it possible to make compact machines such as hairdryers. The motor in a hairdryer works a fan. This blows air across a coil of wire that is heated instantly by electricity, making the air warm.

Perfect toast

A toaster is a machine that heats bread using electric heating elements until it detects that the surface of the bread is hot enough. Then it ejects the toast and turns off the elements.

DOMESTIC HELP

MAKE A CAN CRUSHER

You will need:
*two short planks of wood about
20 inches x 4 inches and ½–1 inch
thick, hinge, screws, screwdriver,
two coffee-jar lids, glue.*

Household machines are designed to make life easier. Here you can make a really useful can crusher and a hand-operated vacuum cleaner. Use the can crusher to flatten empty soda cans before you take them for recycling or to the dump. Crushed cans take up much less space than empty, full-sized ones. This makes them easier to store and to carry.

The crusher is a simple machine that uses a lever action to press on the ends of the can. It is much easier to crush a can with the machine than it is with your hands. The vacuum cleaner is based on the air pump that you have already made. It uses the same principles to pick up scraps of paper as a more sophisticated vacuum cleaner does to pick up household dust. Tissue paper is used for the collection bag because it allows air to pass through it and filters out the scraps of paper. Securing the ping-pong ball to the neck of the pump makes the cleaner more efficient, as it prevents the ball from falling too far out of place.

1 Lay the two planks end to end. Ask an adult to help you screw them together with a hinge, using screws and a screwdriver. Make sure the hinge is secure.

Shredded in seconds
A blender has high-speed chopping blades at the bottom that will cut vegetables and other foods to shreds in seconds. The blades are based on a simple machine: the wedge. Many kitchens are full of gadgets to help make food preparation faster.

2 Glue a jar lid to each plank of wood with the top of the lid face down. The lids should be about halfway along each plank and the same distance from the hinge.

3 To crush a can, put the can in between the lids so that it is held in place. Press down hard on the top piece of wood.

MAKE A VACUUM CLEANER

You will need: *large plastic bottle, scissors, hammer, small nails, wooden stick or dowel, ping-pong ball, string, tape, tissue paper, glue.*

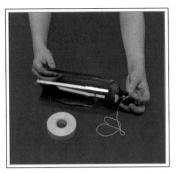

1 Do the air pump project but don't add the valve. Tape string to the ball. Feed the string through the bottle's neck. Tape string to the neck so that the ball falls out a few millimetres.

2 Make a tissue paper bag and glue it over the hole in the bottle. Air from the pump will go through the bag, and anything the vacuum picks up should be trapped.

FACT BOX

• One of the first vacuum cleaners used small pumps like bellows that were attached to the bottom of shoes. The user had to run around to suck up dust!

---

3 Try picking up tiny scraps of paper with the vacuum. Pull the piston out sharply to suck the scraps of paper into the bottle. Push the piston back in gently to pump the paper into the tissue bag. How much can you pick up with your homemade cleaner? Can you pick anything else up, such as grains of salt?

Up the tube
Modern vacuum cleaners have an air pump operated by an electric motor. The pump creates a vacuum inside the cleaner, and dusty air rushes in from the outside to fill the vacuum. A bag at the end of the pipe lets air through but traps dust.

TRANSPORT MACHINES

Bicycles, cars, buses, trucks, trains, ships and aircraft are all machines used for transport. They all make it easier and quicker to travel from one place to another by making use of different types of engines, motors, gears and wheels. The bicycle is one of the most complicated machines that relies on human muscle power to work. A bicycle includes several types of simple machine, such as wheels, axles and levers, and is designed to reduce effort to a minimum.

Larger transport machines have engines and motors to power them. Many also make use of hydraulic, pneumatic and electronic systems. The different systems combine to make the machine efficient, so that it uses the minimum amount of fuel or electricity, and safe, so that there is a low risk of accidents, and passengers are well protected.

Hopalong hobbyhorse
The first bicycles had no gears and no pedals. They were called hobbyhorses, and the riders had to push them along the ground with their feet. They were still quicker than walking.

The gear system allows a cyclist to travel quickly or slowly and still pedal at a comfortable rate.

On your bicycle
A cyclist uses her energy to push down on the pedals. The gear system uses this push to turn the back wheel and drive the bike forward. The tires rub against the road, causing friction, a force that slows things down. Air hitting her body, and her weight, cause her to slow down, too.

The brake lever on the handlebar pulls a cable that makes a brake block press on the wheel rim.

A smooth ride
A pump is used to pump air into the tires. A valve in the tire lets air in, but stops it escaping. Tires are pumped full of air to give a smoother, easier ride.

Electric trains

Overhead cables suspended
above the track provide the
power for the electric
motors that move fast
express trains, such as this
Swedish X2000. Electric
motors work well at low
speeds and high speeds, so
no complicated gears are
needed for the train to speed
up or slow down. Inside the
locomotive cars at each end
of the train are electric
circuits that control the flow
of electricity to the motors.
The driver controls the
speed of the train from the
cab at the front. The train is
also streamlined (shaped to
move smoothly) so that it
cuts easily through the air.

Car parts

All modern cars, from sports cars to
small family cars, have similar
parts. They are moved by an
internal combustion engine
(at the front) which burns
gas or diesel fuel stored in a
tank (at the rear). All the
parts are attached to a steel
body shell.

Aircraft parts

The flaps that extend from an aircraft's
wings to provide extra lift during
take-off and landing are controlled by
hydraulic systems. Airliners, such as this
Airbus A340, are the most complex
transport machines of all, with
thousands of parts. They are moved
through the air by powerful jet engines,
which are complex machines
themselves. Safety is very important, so
most of the aircraft's systems have
back-up systems in case they go wrong.

BUILDING MACHINES

Constructing houses, office parks, bridges, roads and railways involves digging into the ground, moving rock and earth, and transporting and lifting steel, concrete and other heavy building materials. There are specialized construction machines, such as diggers, bulldozers, concrete mixers and cranes, to carry out all these jobs. Many of them use the principles of simple machines to work. For example, cranes use pulleys and balanced levers to help them lift. Most construction machines have large diesel engines to provide the power they need, and some have hydraulic or pneumatic systems to move their parts.

Machinery of old
The Flemish artist Pieter Brueghel painted the mythical Tower of Babel in 1563. It shows the sort of construction machines that were in use in the 1500s, such as chisels, levers, pulleys and simple cranes, operated by large treadmills. The huge cathedrals found in many European cities were built with simple machines like these.

FACT BOX

• The height of a tower crane's tower can be increased. A new section of tower is hauled up and positioned on top of the existing tower.

• Tunnels that go through soft rock, such as chalk, are dug with tunnel boring machines. The machine bores its way through the rock with a rotating cutting head.

• Around 2,000 years ago the Romans used cranes for building. The cranes were powered by slaves walking around in a giant treadmill.

Earth mover
A bulldozer is used to push away rock, soil and rubble to clear a building site ready for work to start. Its wide tracks, called caterpillar tracks, stop it from sinking into muddy ground.

Digging out
A mechanical excavator is used to dig up rock and soil. It makes trenches for pipes, and holes for foundations. Its powerful digging arm is operated by hydraulic rams.

Loading machine

A machine called a loader has a wide bucket that skims along the ground scooping up waste soil. When the bucket is full, hydraulic rams lift it into the air so that the loader can carry it to a waiting dump truck.

Mix it up

A concrete mixer carries concrete to the building site from the factory. Inside the drum a blade, like a screw thread, mixes the concrete. The blade stays still while the drum rotates.

Hammering in

A pile driver hammers piles, or metal posts, into the ground. It repeatedly lifts a large weight with its crane and drops it onto the top of the pile. The piles form the foundation of a new building.

Dumping out

Dump trucks are used to deliver hardcore (crushed up stones used for foundations) and to take away unwanted soil. To empty the load on to the ground, the back of the dump truck is lifted by hydraulic rams. The load slides to the ground.

Towering crane

These tower cranes look flimsy, but they do not topple over even when they are lifting heavy weights. This is because of a concrete counterweight behind the cab.

ON THE FARM

Some of the oldest types of machines in the world are used for agriculture. Farmers use machines to prepare the soil, to sow and harvest their crops, and to feed and milk their animals. One of the first, and still one of the most important farm machines, was the plow. Archaeologists have found evidence of plows from about 9,000 years ago. They began as simple, sharpened sticks that were used to turn up the soil. Today, a seven-furrow plow hauled behind a modern tractor can cover 40 hectares of land—as much as 80 soccer fields—in a day.

Modern farming uses many specialized machines to make cultivated land more productive. In some parts of the world, powered machinery, usually operated by a tractor, does all the work. But in many countries, plows are pulled by animals, and crops are harvested using simple hand tools.

Tractor and plow
Modern, tractor-pulled plows have several individual plows in a row to break up the soil into furrows. This makes it much quicker to plow a field than with a single plow. At the rear end of the tractor is a rotating shaft called a take-off shaft. It provides the power for the plow.

FACT BOX

• On many farms in arid areas, the pumps used to raise water from wells or streams for irrigation, and for animals to drink, are powered by small windmills.

• One of the most important agricultural inventions was the seed drill, which planted seeds in neat rows and at the correct depth. It was invented more than five thousand years ago.

Steam power
Steam-driven traction engines were the first type of tractor. This one was built in 1880. It replaced the farm's horses and powered other machines, such as the thresher shown here.

Animal power
A water buffalo pulls a plow through the soil. Animals, especially oxen, are still widely used by farmers who cannot afford machinery or who live in hilly or mountainous areas.

Pneumatic milking

In a milking parlor, milk is sucked from cows' udders by pneumatic milking machines. A large parlor can milk dozens of cows at the same time. The milk pours into tanks, where it is measured and then pumped to a refrigerated tank to wait for collection by a milk tanker.

Hay wrapper

A baling machine automatically makes hay into bales and wraps them in plastic to keep them dry. Here, the machine is spinning the bale one way as it wraps plastic sheeting around it the other way.

Combine harvester

A combine harvester cuts and collects crops. A reel sweeps the crop into a cutter bar that slices the stalks off at ground level. The stalks are pushed into the machine and the grain is stripped from them. Special screws, called impeller screws or augers, are often used to move the grain around inside the harvester.

A close shave

A sheep farmer uses electrically operated shears to cut the fleece from a sheep. The shears work like a pair of scissors. The electric motor moves the blades together and apart at high speeds.

MAKING FARM MACHINES

The two projects on these pages will show you how to make two simple machines like those used on farms. The first is an Archimedean screw. In parts of the world where water pumps are expensive to buy and run, Archimedean screws are used to move water uphill in order to irrigate crops. The machine is made up of a large screw inside a pipe. One end of the machine is placed in the water and, as a handle is turned, the screw inside revolves, carrying water upward. This water-lifting device has been in use for centuries, and it is named after the ancient Greek scientist, Archimedes.

The second project is to make a simple plow. By pushing the plow through a tray of damp sand you will be able to see how the special, curved, wedge shape of a real plow lifts and turns the soil to make a furrow. A furrow is a trench in which the farmer plants the seeds.

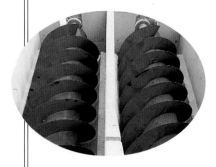

Screwed-up water
Inside an Archimedean screw is a wide screw thread. Water is trapped in the thread and is forced to move upward as the screw is turned. A screw thread like this is also called an auger.

MAKE AN ARCHIMEDEAN SCREW

You will need:
small plastic bottle, scissors, plastic tubing, waterproof tape, two bowls.

1 Cut the top and bottom off the bottle. Wrap a length of plastic tubing around the bottle to make a screw thread shape. Tape the tubing in place with waterproof tape.

2 Put one end of the bottle in a bowl of water and rest it on the bowl's edge. Place the other bowl at the end of the tubing. Slowly turn the bottle. After a few turns, the water will pour out of the top of the tubing.

FACT BOX

• Every year Australian farmers have to shear tens of millions of sheep. As an experiment in 1986, Australian engineers built a robot that could shear a sheep in about 90 seconds.

• The first plows were made from wood or from stag antlers. They were invented in Egypt and India about 5,500 years ago.

MAKE A SIMPLE PLOW

You will need:
small plastic bottle, scissors, strip of wood or dowel, tack, tray of damp sand.

1 Start by cutting a triangle of plastic from one side of the small plastic soda bottle. This triangle will form the blade of your plow.

2 Cut a slot in the triangle, as shown above. Fold the triangle in half along the line of the slot against the curve of the plastic.

3 Holding the two sides of the blade together, attach it to the length of wood or dowel with a tack. Make sure the blade is securely attached to the handle.

Soil-turning wedges
Each metal blade on this plow works as a wedge. The front point slices easily through the soil, splitting it up. As the soil slides along the blade's side, the curved shape lifts and turns it over. The plow buries weeds and brings fresh soil to the surface for new crops to grow in. This is called tilling.

Guided plow
The wheels on a plow from the 1400s stop it from sinking too far into the ground. The farmer guides the plough to make a neat furrow, while a helper urges on oxen and horses.

4 Fill up the tray with damp sand and push the plow through the sand in lines. Does your plow lift and turn the soil to make a furrow?

ELECTRONIC MACHINES

Most of the machines we use have moving parts that are operated by hand or by an engine or motor. These devices are called mechanical machines. Many modern machines, however, such as computers, have no moving parts. They are called electronic machines. Inside an electronic machine lots of components are connected together to form a continuous wire, called a circuit, around which an electric current flows. The components control the way electricity flows around the circuits and so control what the machine does. Complicated electronic circuits, containing hundreds of thousands of components, can be contained on a single microchip a few millimetres across.

Some electronic machines, such as weighing scales and digital watches, do the same job as mechanical machines. Many modern machines, such as robots, are combinations of mechanical and electronic parts.

Weighing scale
When an orange is put on a scale, it presses on an electronic device called a strain gauge. The gauge controls the strength of a tiny electric current. Electronics inside the machine detect the size of the current, determine the orange's weight, and show it on a display panel to be read.

Internet on the phone
A cellphone is an extremely complex machine in a tiny case. It is a combination of a telephone and radio receiver and transmitter. As well as being a phone, this machine can send and receive e-mails, and download web pages from the Internet and display them on its screen.

Palm-top computer
The personal digital assistant (PDA) is a small but powerful type of electronic machine. It is a palm-sized computer that stores personal data.

Microscopic microchips
A photomicrograph (a photograph taken through a microscope) shows the tiny components on a microchip, each too small to see with the naked eye. The chip starts as a thin layer of silicon, and the components are built up using complex chemical and photographic processes.

The first computers

One of the first electronic computers was called ENIAC (Electronic Numeral Integrator And Calculator). It was built in the 1940s. It took up a huge amount of space because its electronic parts were thousands of times bigger than today's microchips. ENIAC needed several rooms to fit in all its valves, wires and dials, but it was less powerful than a modern pocket calculator.

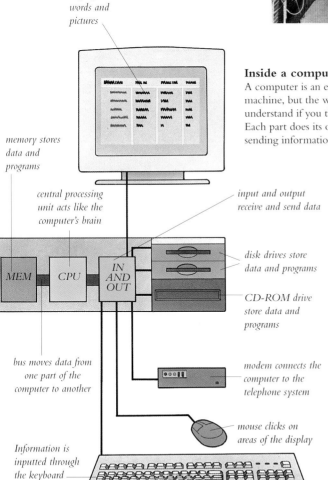

display shows words and pictures

Inside a computer system

A computer is an extremely complicated machine, but the way it works is quite easy to understand if you think of it in several parts. Each part does its own job, such as storing or sending information.

memory stores data and programs

central processing unit acts like the computer's brain

input and output receive and send data

disk drives store data and programs

MEM   CPU   IN AND OUT

CD-ROM drive store data and programs

bus moves data from one part of the computer to another

modem connects the computer to the telephone system

mouse clicks on areas of the display

Information is inputted through the keyboard

MACHINES IN INDUSTRY

In a spin
A steam-powered circular saw is used to cut large logs into shape. The saw has a razor-sharp blade with teeth that cut into the material as it spins. The object that is being cut is moved backward or forward across the blade.

Machine tools are machines used in factories to manufacture objects. The operations they are used for are cutting, drilling, grinding, turning and milling. Each of these operations is done by a special machine. For example, the operation of turning (forming a curve in the material) is done on a lathe, and cutting is done with a saw. All machine tools have a cutting blade or edge, which is normally made of metal, but may include diamond or other tough materials. The blade moves against the object being cut, called the workpiece, shaving off unwanted material.

Machine tools are used to make engine parts and other complex machines in which the parts have to fit together perfectly. Industrial robots are versatile machines that can be programmed to do many jobs, such as moving workpieces or drilling very accurately.

Pedal power
A pole lathe is powered by a foot-operated pedal. The lathe spins the workpiece around very fast. The operator presses cutting tools against the spinning wood, shaving off a layer each time. How accurately the workpiece is finished depends on the skill of the lathe operator.

A perfect fit
Under computer control, this miniature milling machine is shaping a piece of ceramic material so that it will fit perfectly into a cavity in a dental patient's tooth. A milling machine cuts out areas of a piece of material. The cutting tool has rotating teeth, similar to a gear wheel.

Pressed panels
A machine called a die press flattens sheets of steel into shaped panels, such as those used for car hoods. The top part of the machine moves down to press the panel into shape. Each sheet of steel is pressed into exactly the same shape every time.

Digital control

An engineer makes a heating element from a graphite rod using a computer-controlled milling machine. Data describing the shape and size of the heating element is fed into the machine's computer, normally from another computer on which it has been designed. The computer then determines the cutting movements required to make the heating element from the rod and operates the milling machine very precisely.

Keeping cool

The milky liquid pouring onto this drill is, in fact, colored water. As the drill bit cuts into the metal workpiece, it gets very hot. The water keeps the drill cool, stopping the tool from melting and washing away waste metal.

Industrial robots

Robots are used for welding car components together. The robot is shown how to do the job once and can then do it over and over again, much faster than a human worker.

FACT BOX

• In some industries, high-energy lasers are used for cutting and shaping materials instead of traditional machine tools. The most powerful lasers can cut through 2½ inches of steel.

• In some car-making factories, parts for the cars are delivered by robot vehicles that are programmed to drive themselves around the floor of the factory.

MACHINES OF THE FUTURE

Machines that do complicated jobs need controls. Some of these machines need a human operator who controls the machine manually. For example, a car needs a driver to control its speed and direction. Other machines control themselves—once they are turned on, they do their job automatically. For example, an automatic washing machine washes and spins your clothes at the press of a button. One of the first machines to use a form of automatic control was the Jacquard loom. Punched paper cards were fed into the loom and told it which threads were to be used. Today, many machines are controlled by computer to perform a set task whenever it is required. The most advanced machines are even able to check their own work and change it if necessary.

Flying by wires
Airliners and fighter aircraft may have a "fly-by-wire" control system, where a computer, rather than the pilot, actually flies the plane. The pilot monitors how the plane is working by watching a computer screen instead of dials.

Journey through space
Shuttle-like space planes, such as the experimental X-33, will eventually be used to transport passengers via space. Space planes could reduce the usual flight time from New York to Tokyo from nearly 14 hours to just a couple of hours.

Robotic rover
A toy robot dog has built-in artificial intelligence. It knows nothing at first, but it gradually figures out the layout of its new home and learns to respond to its new owner's commands.

Tiny machine
The rotor in this photograph is actually only about 0.5mm across. It is part of a meter that measures liquid flow. It is made of silicon and was manufactured using similar methods to those used to make microchips. Tiny machines such as this are called micromachines.

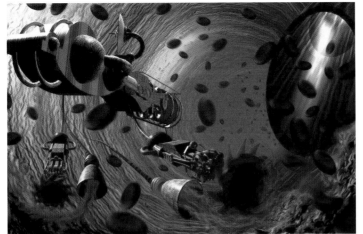

Robotic surgeon

In the future, it is possible that microscopic machines will be used in surgery. In this futuristic painting a microscopic robot is repairing a human body. The robot, just 0.1mm long, has been injected into a blood vessel through the needle on the right. Around the robot are red blood cells. With its rotating blades, the robot is cutting away a blockage made of debris (shown in gray). The robot sucks up the debris for removal.

Invisible gears

These gear wheels look quite ordinary, but they were made using microscopic experimental technology called nanotechnology. The width of the wheels is less than the width of a human hair. A hundred of these gear wheels piled up would be only as tall as the thickness of a sheet of paper!

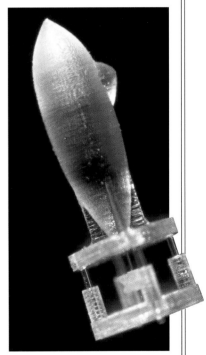

Handy android

An android (a human–like robot) uses electronic eyes and ears to figure out where objects are and its hand to pick them up. With its artificial intelligence, it can decide what kind of object it is holding. Androids help scientists to research how robots can be made to act like humans.

Car control

Many of this car's systems are controlled by a microchip called a microprocessor. It continually checks signals from sensors and sends a control signal back again. It calculates the speed, distance and fuel consumption of the car and displays them on the dashboard.

Mini submarine

A miniature submarine that measures just 4mm from top to bottom was made using an experimental technique for creating microscopic machine parts. The technique uses tiny laser beams to solidify selected parts of a pool of liquid plastic to form the submarine's shape.

AUTOMATIC CONTROL

CONTROLING A ROBOT

You will need:
blindfold, egg and egg-cup.

Machines that perform very difficult, complicated tasks need to be controlled with precision. Robots are machines that are programmed with instructions for different situations. They can respond to each situation in an 'intelligent' way, rather like human beings. However, although robots seem to be very clever, they can only do what they are told to do. The project below will show you how tricky it is to program a robot to do even the simplest job. Using only the words that are from the list of commands, see if a friend can carry out the task successfully.

The second project shows you how to make a simple control disc. This is the sort of device used to control some washing machines. The metal track on the disc is part of an electric circuit. As the disc turns, the track completes or breaks the circuit, turning parts of the machine, such as lights and motors, on and off.

Robot commands
FORWARD
STOP
TURN LEFT
TURN RIGHT
ARM UP
ARM DOWN
CLOSE FINGERS
OPEN FINGERS

1 Ask a friend to put on the blindfold. Use the list of commands opposite to direct your friend to where the egg is located.

2 Your friend should not know where the egg is or what to do with it. Instruct your friend to carefully pick the egg up. Only use commands in the list.

3 Now ask your friend to accurately place the egg on another surface. See if your friend can put it in the egg-cup. How quickly was your friend able to complete the task? The faster your friend completes the task, the better you are at programming.

MAKE A CONTROL DISC

You will need: compass and pencil, ruler, cardboard, scissors, aluminum pie pan, glue, tape, paper fastener, wire, three plastic-coated wires, battery, flashlight bulb and holder.

1 Use a compass to mark out a 4 inch disc of cardboard and cut it out. Also cut a 2½ inch ring from the foil dish and glue it onto the cardboard.

2 Put pieces of tape across the foil track. The bare foil will complete the circuit. The pieces of tape will break the circuit.

Loom control

The Jacquard loom, invented in 1801, was one of the first machines with automatic control. Cards with patterns of holes in them, called punched cards, controlled how threads were woven together to create patterns in the fabric that the loom made. The pattern created could be changed simply by changing to another set of cards with a different pattern of holes.

3 Push a paper fastener through the middle of the disc and mount it onto a piece of cardboard. Using the wire, make two contacts with a bend in the middle, as shown.

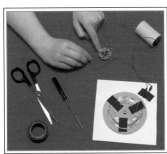

4 Stick the contacts to the cardboard so they press on the foil. Connect a battery to a bulb with plastic-coated wire. Attach a second piece of plastic-coated wire to the bulb, and a third to the battery.

5 Attach the two loose wires to the two contacts on the cardboard. You have now made a circuit. Turn the disc slowly. The light bulb goes on and off as the disc turns. As the contacts go over a piece of tape, the circuit is broken and the light goes out. When they touch the foil again, the circuit is completed and the light comes back on.

GLOSSARY

auger
A large tool shaped like a corkscrew, for boring holes in the ground.

ax
A wedge of metal on the end of a long handle, which is used to split wood.

axle
A bar that joins wheels together. Axles turn on bearings.

belt drive
A device that uses a belt to transfer a drive from one pulley to another. Many sewing machines have belt drives.

bevelled gears
Gears with teeth set at an angle. These gears are usually set at right angles to each other and change the direction of the drive.

bionic machine
A machine that acts like a living thing.

block and tackle
A device that uses two sets of pulley blocks to help raise very heavy weights.

capstan wheel
A revolving barrel in which the effort is applied by pushing against long horizontal levers. Capstans were used to raise anchors on ships.

chain drive
A device that uses a chain to transfer a drive from one gear wheel to another, such as on a bicycle.

chisel
A metal cutting tool with a wedge at its edge.

compressed air
Air that has been squashed into a smaller volume than usual.

construction machine
A machine, such as a digger, that is used on building sites.

crankshaft
An axle that has parts of it bent at right angles so that the up and down motion of pistons is turned into circular motion.

die press
A machine that squeezes metal into a shape using great force.

drill
A cutting tool that has a spiral blade for removing waste material.

driveshaft
The bar that is turned by an engine to drive wheels.

effort
The force applied to a lever or other simple machine to move a load.

electronic circuit
A circuit that consists of transistors.

e-mail
A method of sending messages between computers.

engine
A device that provides turning power.

first class lever
A simple lever such as a see-saw, in which the pivot is between the two ends.

force
A push or a pull which results in an object moving faster or slower.

gear
A wheel that has teeth that mesh with another gearwheel's teeth.

gearbox
A set of gearwheels of different sizes that can turn wheels at different speeds and with different mechanical advantages.

gravity
The pulling force that operates between all masses.

groove
A channel cut in a pulley wheel to keep a belt drive in place.

hydraulics
The use of water or other liquids to move pistons and other devices.

hydroelectric power
Power derived from moving water.

inclined plane
A slope up which heavy objects can be moved more easily than by raising them vertically.

internal combustion engine
A motor that burns gas or diesel in cylinders, to supply hot gases to push pistons.

laser
A device that produces an intense beam of light.

lathe
A machine that spins an object against a cutting tool.

lever
A long bar that is used against a pivot to help move a heavy object.

load
The weight moved by a lever or other machine.

lock
A device to prevent something, such as a door, from opening.

mains power
Electricity supplied to homes from power stations.

mass
The amount of material in an object. Mass is measured in pounds and ounces.

mechanical advantage
The number of times by which the load is greater than the effort.

microchip
A device that has thousands of electronic circuits on a sliver of silicon.

micromachine
A very small machine.

mill
To grind or cut metal, stone, or wood using a machine with a turning motion.

nanotechnology
The study of how to make and use micromachines and other tiny devices.

nut
A piece of metal, usually hexagonal, that fits onto a screw.

pendulum
A swinging mass hanging from a thread or bar, found in old-fashioned clocks, to help keep regular time.

piston
A disc or cylinder that fits snugly inside another cylinder, but is still able to move up and down.

pivot
The point about which a lever turns.

plow
A large blade that cuts through soil and turns it over.

pneumatics
The use of air or other gases to move pistons and other devices.

pulley
A wheel over which a rope or chain can be slung to help move heavy objects.

ramp
See inclined plane.

ratchet
A device that allows movement in one direction only.

rotor
A device that rotates on its axis such as the rotor blade of a helicopter.

screw
A spiral thread on a metal bar that can be used in a jack to help raise a load.

screw jack
A device that uses a screw to help raise a weight from below.

screwdriver
A device for turning screws.

second class lever
A lever, such as a wheelbarrow, in which the pivot is at the end of the bar.

silicon
A non-metal which, as an oxide, forms quartz.

simple machine
A device used to help in doing work.

spanner
A device that grips a nut. The spanner's handle works like a lever to help turn the nut.

spoke
A piece of metal that joins the rim of a wheel to the hub.

third class lever
A lever in which the effort is applied between the pivot and the load.

tooth
The part of a gear wheel that fits into a chain in a chain drive.

treadmill
A wheel that can be turned by an animal or a person walking on the inner rim of the wheel.

turbine
A motor in which the turning force is supplied by water or gases pushing on a series of vanes or propelers.

turning
A twisting or rotating motion.

valve
A device that allows liquids or gases to flow in one direction only.

web page
Information that is set up on a computer to be viewed by other people using their own computers.

wedge
An object, such as an ax head, which is thin at one end and wider at the other.

INDEX

PICTURE CREDITS
b=bottom, t=top, c=center, l=left, r=right

Ancient Art and Architecture Collection Ltd: page 8. Ancient Egypt Picture Library: page 18t&b. Aviation Photographs International: page 37c. Barnaby's Picture Library/Gerald Clyde page 25bl. Bruce Coleman Ltd: pages 32bl&r, 33t; /Massimo Borchi page 15c; /Janos Jurka page 11; /Harald Lange page 5tr; /Neil McAllister page 62; /H P Merten page 57bl. Ecoscene: pages 32t, 49bl; /Gryniewicz page 56bl; /Nick Hawkes pages 19tr, 48bl; /W Lawler page 20bl; /M Maidment page 51b; /Sally Morgan page 16; /Towse page 52. E.T. Archive: pages 15t, 24, 46, 48t, 53, 55. Mary Evans Picture Library: page 29b. Holt Studios International: /Ivan Belcher pages 50bl, 58br; /Nigel Cattlin pages 48br, 50br, 51c; /Paul McCullagh page 7; /Primrose Peacock page 56t; /Inga Spence page 51t. ICCE/Mark Boulton page 5bl. Image Bank: pages 15b, 19b. Planet Earth Pictures: pages 19tl; 63br. Quadrant: pages 25br, 37t, 47b; /Auto Express page 59b; /Anthony R Dalton page 47t; /Bryn Williams page 63bl. Science Museum/Science & Society Picture Library: page 43t&b. Science Photo Library: page 58t; /Dr Jeremy Burgess page 63tr; /Vaughan Fleming page 29c; /Food & Drug Administration page 56br; /Adam Hart-Davis page 25t; /Sheila Terry page 57t; /Rosenfeld Images Ltd pages 57bl, 59tl; /David Parker page 58bl. Superstock: pages 5tl, 49br. Tony Stone: pages 39t, 47c. Trip: /Joynson-Hicks page 36t; /H Rogers pages 10, 49tr&l. Zefa: pages 5br, 20br, 33bl&r, 36b, 39b, 54, 59tr, 63tl; /Dieter Pittius page 26.